SOCCER
RECORD BREAKERS

BY NICK HUNTER

CAPSTONE PRESS
a capstone imprint

Published by Capstone Press, an imprint of Capstone
1710 Roe Crest Drive, North Mankato, Minnesota 56003
capstonepub.com

Copyright © 2025 by Capstone. All rights reserved. No part of this publication may be reproduced in whole or in part, or stored in a retrieval system, or transmitted in any form or by any means, electronic, mechanical, photocopying, recording, or otherwise, without written permission of the publisher.

SPORTS ILLUSTRATED KIDS is a trademark of ABG-SI LLC. Used with permission.

Library of Congress Cataloging-in-Publication Data is available on the Library of Congress website.
ISBN: 9781669076001 (hardcover)
ISBN: 9781669075950 (paperback)
ISBN: 9781669075967 (ebook pdf)

Summary: With billions of fans and giant stadiums packed with cheering crowds, soccer itself is record-breaking. Find out even more by reading about soccer's record-breaking superstar players, trophy-winning teams, and standout coaches.

Editor: Erika L. Shores; Designer: Sofiia Rovinskaia; Media Researcher: Jo Miller; Production Specialist: Tori Abraham

Image Credits
Alamy: Sueddeutsche Zeitung Photo, 11, tony quinn, 15, Xinhua, 29; Getty Images: Alex Grimm, 21, Alexander Hassenstein, 14, Alexandre Schneider, 12, CLEMENT MAHOUDEAU, 18, Clive Brunskill, 5, Fran Santiago, 7, Lars Baron, 25, NurPhoto, 27, Pedro Vilela, 9, Ronald Martinez, 8; Shutterstock: cristiano barni, 13, FocusStocker, Cover, (top), ph.FAB, 17, 23, Volodymyr Maksymchuk, 19; Sports Illustrated: Erick W. Rasco, Cover, (bottom both), Simon Bruty, 10

Design Elements: Shutterstock: Gojindbefs, Kucher Serhii (football), Lifestyle Graphic, Navin Penrat

Any additional websites and resources referenced in this book are not maintained, authorized, or sponsored by Capstone. All product and company names are trademarks™ or registered® trademarks of their respective holders.

TABLE OF CONTENTS

A Record-Breaking Sport 4
Giants of the Game 6
Top Teams 20
Big Crowds and Big Money 26

    Glossary 30
    Read More 31
    Internet Sites 31
    Index 32
    About the Author 32

Words in **BOLD** are in the glossary.

A RECORD-BREAKING SPORT

Soccer is the most popular sport in more than 200 countries around the world. The sport is played by more than 250 million people and followed by more than 3.5 billion supporters. The world's biggest sport is truly a record breaker.

Many young players dream of scoring the winning goal in a World Cup final or lifting the **league** title for their favorite team. The very best players and teams go further. They want to play more games, win more trophies, and score more goals. In the process, they become soccer record breakers. Fans can discuss who are the most skillful or most exciting players. Record breakers have numbers or statistics on their side to show they are the best.

Lionel Messi holds up the trophy after he and his teammates from Argentina won the 2022 World Cup.

GIANTS OF THE GAME

Soccer is a team game, but some players' names are more widely known than the teams they play for. These players are the giants of the game. They are known for their long careers and the amazing number of trophies they have won.

MOST TROPHIES

Players who are good enough to play for the best teams for many successful years win a lot of trophies. In 2023, Lionel Messi claimed the record for winning the most trophies when his team Inter Miami won the Leagues Cup. It was his 44th trophy. Many of them were won in his long career for Barcelona.

Lionel Messi (with trophy) and FC Barcelona won Copa del Rey in 2021.

APPEARANCE RECORDS

Playing for their national team is a proud moment for any player. Some players are picked for their country's team year after year. Top of the list is Kristine Lilly, who played 354 times for the U.S. Women's National team. The "Queen of **Caps**" also scored 130 goals between 1987 and 2010.

Kristine Lilly

Portuguese superstar Cristiano Ronaldo holds the record for **international** caps by a male player. He has more than 200 appearances. Not all record breakers are as famous. Just behind Ronaldo is Bader Al-Mutawa of Kuwait. He retired in 2022 having played 196 times for his country.

Brazilian goalkeeper Rogério Ceni stands out as a record breaker in club soccer. His 1,238 games for São Paulo is a record for one club. On top of that, Ceni also holds the record for most goals by a goalkeeper with 131 strikes.

Rogério Ceni

INDIVIDUAL AWARDS

Most trophies are won by teams, but there are some awards for individuals. Every year, soccer's governing body, FIFA, names a Best Men's and a Best Women's Player. Two players have **dominated** this award. Lionel Messi has won seven times while brilliant Brazilian women's star Marta has won six times. Will their records ever be broken?

Marta

Pelé

YOUNGEST AND OLDEST

For some great players, World Cup success comes very early or late in their careers. The youngest World Cup winner became one of soccer's greatest players. Pelé was 17 years and 249 days old when Brazil won in 1958. He is also the only player with three World Cup winner's medals. Italian goalkeeper and captain Dino Zoff is the oldest player to win the World Cup. He lifted the trophy in 1982 at the age of 40.

ULTIMATE GOAL-SCORERS

Goals win games. Soccer matches are often decided by one or two goals. Players who get the ball in the back of the net are adored by fans and are key parts of any team.

The leading international goal-scorer of all time is Christine Sinclair of Canada. As she prepared for the 2023 Women's World Cup, "Sinc" had scored 190 international goals in an amazing career. That's just ahead of Abby Wambach's 184 goals for the U.S. between 2001 and 2015.

Christine Sinclair

Portugal's Cristiano Ronaldo collects goal-scoring records. Ronaldo began his career as a skillful **midfielder** but soon showed his goal-scoring skills. Ronaldo has scored more international goals than any other male player with 123. His 140 goals in Europe's Champions League is also a record. Most people agree Ronaldo has scored more top-level goals than any other player.

Cristiano Ronaldo

WORLD CUP RECORD BREAKERS

The World Cup is the biggest stage for any goal-scorer, when the pressure to score is higher than ever. The record for goals scored in Men's World Cup **tournaments** is 16, held by Germany's Miroslav Klose. Klose's strikes helped his team win the World Cup in 2014.

Miroslav Klose

Archie Thompson of Australia has scored the most goals in a single international game. Thompson grabbed 13 goals in one match against American Samoa in 2001. The final score was 31–0.

Brazil's Marta holds the record for the Women's World Cup with 17 goals scored at five different competitions. U.S. striker Michelle Akers scored an amazing 10 goals in the first women's tournament in 1991.

Michelle Akers

MOST GOALS IN A YEAR

There are hundreds of different soccer leagues around the world with their own goal-scoring records. Official records usually list Lionel Messi as record goal-scorer in a year with 91 goals in 2012. He may have to take second place to the striking total of Zambia's Godfrey Chitalu. In 1972, Chitalu scored 107 goals in 50 matches playing for Kabwe Warriors and Zambia. His record included 18 **hat tricks** along with seven goals in a single match.

FUTURE RECORD BREAKER

Which goal scorers will be the record breakers of the future? Erling Haaland joined Manchester City in 2022. He scored a record 52 goals as the team won the English Premier League, European Champions League, and FA Cup in his first season. Haaland could be breaking records for many years to come.

Erling Haaland lifts the trophy after his team, Manchester City, won the Champions League in 2023.

RED CARD RECORDS

Not all players are proud of the records they achieve. Most players want to avoid being shown a red card by the referee and sent off the pitch. The quickest sending off in soccer history could be the red card shown to Jean-Clair Todibo of French club Nice. Todibo was sent off for fouling an opposing player after just nine seconds in a league game in 2022.

Jean-Clair Todibo speaks with officials after receiving a red card.

In 2011, the teams Claypole and Victoriano Arenas set an unwanted record. After a fight broke out, referee Damian Rubino started showing red cards to calm things down. He ended up sending off 36 people including all players, **substitutes**, and coaches for both teams.

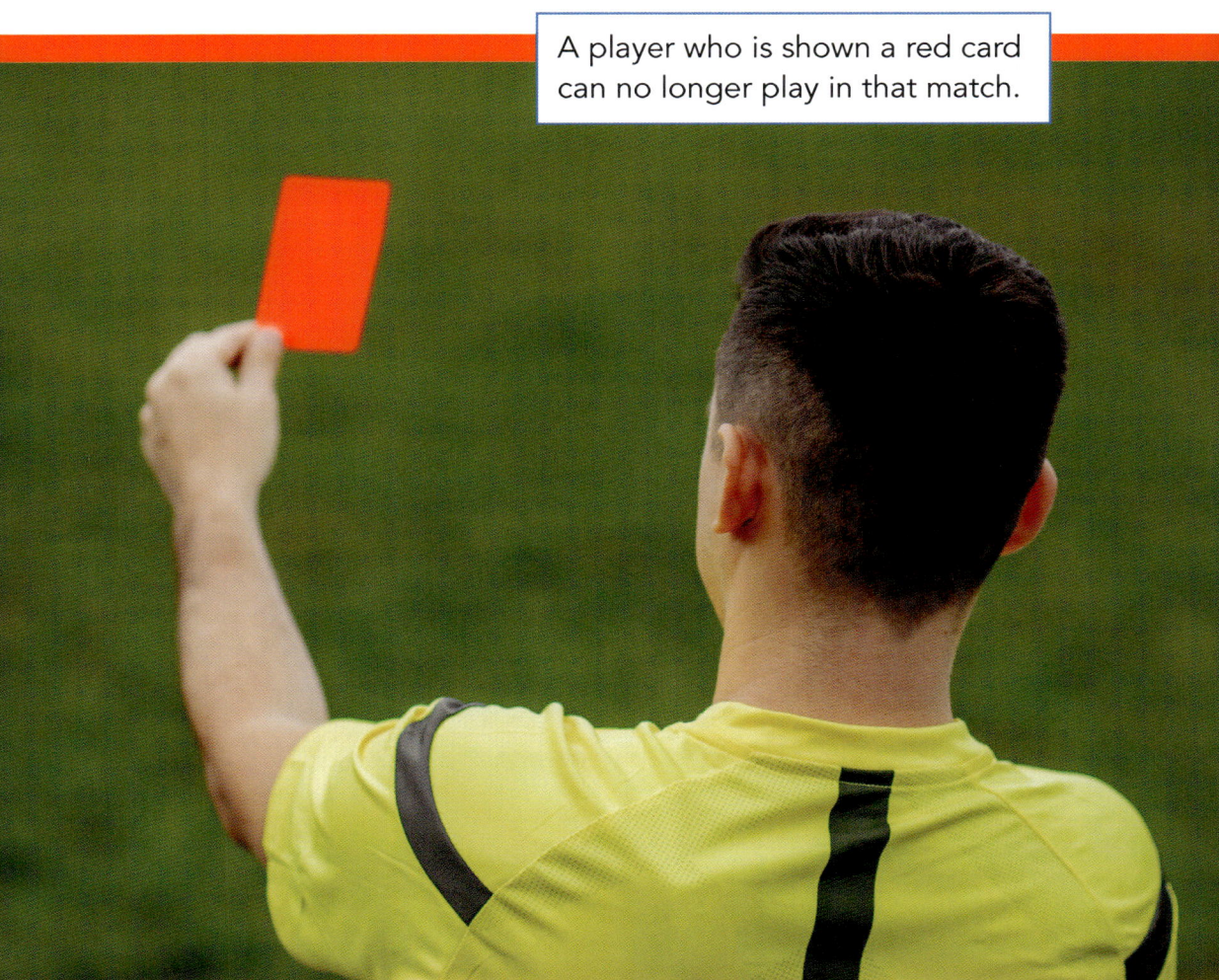

A player who is shown a red card can no longer play in that match.

TOP TEAMS

Record-breaking teams keep on being successful even though their players change.

TOP NATIONS

The best national teams meet at the World Cup tournament every four years. The most successful country in men's World Cups is Brazil. The skillful South Americans have won the trophy five times with a changing team of star players such as Pelé, Romário, and Ronaldo. Germany (previously West Germany) has played in the World Cup final a record eight times, winning it four times.

The United States is the most successful nation in Women's World Cup, winning four times. The U.S. team has featured many star players over the years, including Mia Hamm, Carli Lloyd, and Megan Rapinoe.

For some teams just **qualifying** for the tournament is a big deal. The smallest country ever to reach the World Cup is Iceland, which is home to about 350,000 people. Iceland played in the 2018 World Cup in Russia.

Megan Rapinoe (with trophy) and the U.S. team celebrate their World Cup win in 2019.

CHAMPION CLUBS

The European Champions League is played between the top teams from different leagues. The winning club is the best team in Europe. Spain's Real Madrid won the first five trophies between 1956 and 1960 (when the trophy was called the European Cup). The club holds the record for winning the trophy 14 times. Real Madrid also has the most wins in the Club World Cup, which includes the best club teams from around the world.

The Isles of Scilly off the coast of the United Kingdom is home to 2,000 people. The islands' soccer league holds the record for the fewest clubs. Two clubs play each other around 20 times each season.

Real Madrid won the Champions League on May 28, 2022.

23

WINNING MANAGERS

Successful managers and coaches are behind every championship team. Sir Alex Ferguson is the most successful manager of all time with 49 trophies for Scottish club Aberdeen and Manchester United between 1980 and 2013.

PLAYERS AND MANAGERS

Three men have lifted the World Cup as both player and manager. Mário Zagallo played on the winning Brazil teams of 1958 and 1962, and he managed the team in 1970. Franz Beckenbauer captained West Germany in 1974 and managed in 1990. Didier Deschamps played for France in 1998. Deschamps came close to winning twice as a manager. After his France team won in 2018, they lost in the final in 2022.

When teams are losing matches, they are quick to fire the manager. Leroy Rosenior was manager of English club Torquay United for just 10 minutes before new owners decided they wanted someone else.

Didier Deschamps at the World Cup in 2022

BIG CROWDS AND BIG MONEY

While the players break records on the pitch, soccer crowds and stadiums are also setting new records.

BIGGEST STADIUMS

Soccer can be played on almost any area of flat ground, but the most popular teams play their matches in front of huge cheering crowds. Europe's biggest soccer stadium is the Camp Nou in Barcelona, Spain. It can seat almost 100,000 people.

In the past, crowds were often even bigger because stadiums allowed standing supporters. The 1950 World Cup final in Maracaña Stadium, Rio de Janeiro, between Brazil and Uruguay was watched by 173,850 fans.

Crowds at women's soccer matches are getting bigger every year. In 2022, the Camp Nou stadium welcomed a record crowd of 91,648 to watch Barcelona's women's team against Germany's Wolfsburg.

A record crowd filled the Camp Nou stadium to watch Barcelona's women's team beat Germany's Wolfsburg on April 22, 2022.

RECORD AUDIENCES

Big tournaments such as the World Cup also attract record TV audiences. About 1.5 billion people around the world watched the 2022 World Cup final between Argentina and France. Earlier in the tournament, the United States played England. This match was watched by more people in English and Spanish than any other men's soccer match in U.S. history. Record TV audiences also watched the 2023 Women's World Cup. These record audiences include kids watching the world's greatest players for the first time. Are soccer's record breakers of the future among these young fans?

RECORD REWARDS

Big audiences mean big money. In 2022, the three highest paid athletes in the world were all soccer players. They were Cristiano Ronaldo, Lionel Messi, and Kylian Mbappé. Estimated earnings for each player were more than $120 million.

France's Kylian Mbappé was one of the standout soccer stars audiences watched during the 2022 World Cup.

GLOSSARY

cap (CAP)—appearance for a national team

dominate (DOM-uh-nayt)—have power over

hat trick (HAT TRIK)—when a player scores three goals in a match

international (in-tur-NASH-uh-nuhl)—including more than one country

league (LEEG)—a group of teams who play against each other regularly

midfielder (mid-FEEL-dur)—a player who plays between defenders and forwards

qualify (KWAL-uh-fye)—appear at a tournament by winning matches against others

substitute (SUB-stuh-toot)—a player who replaces another player during a match

tournament (TOUR-nuh-ment)—a series of games that make up a competition

READ MORE

Hewson, Anthony K. *GOATs of Soccer.* Minneapolis: ABDO SportsZone, 2022.

Kerry, Isaac. *What You Never Knew About Lionel Messi.* North Mankato, MN: Capstone, 2023.

Schwartz, Heather E. *U.S. Women's National Soccer Team: Winning On and Off the Field.* Minneapolis: Lerner Publishing, 2024.

INTERNET SITES

ESPN: Soccer Leagues and Competitions
espn.com/soccer/competitions

Sports Illustrated Kids: Soccer
sikids.com/tag/soccer

U.S. Soccer
ussoccer.com

INDEX

Akers, Michelle, 15
Al-Mutawa, Bader, 9

Beckenbauer, Franz, 24

Camp Nou, 26, 27
Ceni, Rogério, 9
Champions League, 16, 17, 22, 23
Chitalu, Godfrey, 16

Deschamps, Didier, 24, 25

Ferguson, Sir Alex, 24

Haaland, Erling, 16, 17
Hamm, Mia, 20

Klose, Miroslav, 14

Lilly, Kristine, 8

Maracaña Stadium, 26
Marta, 10, 15
Mbappé, Kylian, 28, 29
Messi, Lionel, 5, 6, 7, 10, 16, 28

Pelé, 11, 20
Premier League, 16

Rapinoe, Megan, 20, 21
Ronaldo, Cristiano, 9, 13, 20, 28
Rosenior, Leroy, 24
Rubino, Damian, 19

Sinclair, Christine, 12

Thompson, Archie, 14
Todibo, Jean-Clair, 18

Wambach, Abby, 12
Women's World Cup, 12, 15, 20, 21, 28
World Cup, 4, 5, 11, 14, 20, 21, 24, 25, 28, 29

Zagallo, Mário, 24
Zoff, Dino, 11

ABOUT THE AUTHOR

Nick Hunter has written more than 100 books for young people. He specializes in writing about history, social studies, and sports. Nick lives in Oxford, UK, with his wife and two sports-loving sons. His favorite soccer teams are Norwich City and England.